HYGGE & SP[OOKY]

SUPER CUTE AND FUN ADULT

DK

Hygge (pronounced "hyoo-guh") is a beautiful Danish concept that celebrates the warmth of togetherness and the calm comfort of being fully present. **HYGGE SPOOKY** puts a charming twist on this idea, inviting you into a whimsical Halloween world filled with creepy-cute fun and heartwarming calm. Wander through pumpkin-lit paths, haunted hideouts and ghostly gardens alongside our adorable animal friends - each one enjoying the softer, sweeter side of the spooky season. This is not your typical season - it is Halloween the hygge way.

THIS BOOK BELONGS TO

BEFORE YOU START...

Dear Creative Maestros,

To ensure the best coloring experience, please consider the following tips:

- The paper in this book is well-suited for colored pencils.

- If you are using alcohol-based markers, to prevent any bleed-through and protect the page underneath, we recommend placing a piece of thick paper or card stock behind the paper you are coloring.

This simple step will help keep the rest of your book clean and ensure your artwork remains pristine.

Happy Coloring !

Use Blank Thick Sheet of Paper
or
Use Card Stock

TEST COLOR PAGE

SHARE WITH US

We would love to see your amazing coloring creations!

Share your beautiful masterpiece on **Instagram** and **Tik Tok**, and tag us **@SuiSui_Coloring**. Whether you are bringing to life the cozy scenes or adding vibrant flair to the pages, we can't wait to feature and celebrate your work. Use the tag **#SuiSui_Coloring** for chance to be featured in our stories and posts.

Join the fun in our **Facebook** group: **Sui Sui Coloring Community**, where you can connect, share, and be inspired. Let's spread Creativity and Love together!

Instagram QR Code

Facebook Group QR Code

Tik Tok QR Code

FREE BONUSES FOR YOU

Dear Creative Maestros,

We know how much joy coloring brings. If you don't want the fun to stop and if you have finished this book but you are not ready to part with this Super Cute and Fun Creatures yet, we've got **Free Bonuses For You**.

What Do You Get for Free?

- Additional Coloring pages with Super Cute and Fun Creatures
  BONUS 1: $10.00 - **FREE 8+ pages**
  BONUS 2: $15.00 - **FREE 35+ pages**
  BONUS 3: $15.00 - **FREE 35+ pages**
  BONUS 4: $15.00 - **FREE 34+ pages**
  BONUS 5: $10.00 - **FREE 10+ pages**
  BONUS 6: $15.00 - **FREE 40+ pages**
  BONUS 7: $15.00 - **FREE 40+ pages**
  Total: $95.00 - FREE 202+ pages

- Extended Enjoyment and Fun to keep your creativity buzzing

Use camera on your phone,
then Scan the code,
Click the Link

Where Do You Get the Free Bonuses?

https://suisuibooks.com/free-gift201   or

SUI SUI

CAN WE ASK FOR A TINY FAVOR?

THANK YOU for picking up this book and joining me in this fun - artistic adventure.

If you have enjoyed our Coloring Book, I have a personal tiny favor to ask:

Could you please take moment right now and leave a review on Amazon?
It will only take less than **60 seconds**

Your feedback is incredibly valuable - it is like the lifeblood for a small independent author like me. By sharing your thoughts, you are contributing significantly to my publishing journey.

Your review will also help others discover the joy of coloring and support my work in a meaningful way. People do judge a book by its reviews. That **one minute** of your time can truly make a world of difference to me. Thank you very much in advance.

To leave the review for Hygge Spooky:
   1. Pick 1x Amazon store where you purchased the book from:

USA	UK	Canada	Australia	France.	Netherlands

   2. Use camera on your phone, Scan the Code, click the link, leave the review

Printed in Dunstable, United Kingdom